CW00421129

COI

KAIROS: OUR BEGINNINGS

Kairos Church was planted by John and Laura Caldwell in 2020. The pioneering journey began in January when they were prayed for and sent out from their local church to begin a fresh ministry in the Stirling area.

There were a number of prophetic words that led to both the planting of Kairos and the alignment with the Apostolic church. The late Larry Donaldson (Glasgow City Church) prophesied that God was going to raise up a fresh work in Stirling, it would be a long work (it would take time to establish), the roots and foundations would be deep, and from this work a number of other churches would be planted.

Initially we started monthly Encounter evenings and a small group in our home. By March 2020 the Covid 19 pandemic shut everything down and we had to go into lockdown. During this time we continued to meet as small group on Zoom, and we began to lay the foundations for establishing a local church. We officially launched Kairos in May 2020, and in September 2020 John was ordained by the Apostolic Church UK as the lead pastor and Kairos was incorporated into the Apostolic Church.

We are excited about what we have seen God do over

the last few years, what he is doing just now, and what he will do in the future.

Our heart is to be a church that impacts Stirling and beyond. We are passionate about Jesus, and the call to follow him and see others transformed by his grace. Our heart is to know Jesus and make him known. We long to see lives transformed as they encounter Jesus, follow him and lead others to him.

This handbook has been designed for those who are new to Kairos Church, and also emerging leaders. It's a snapshot of the DNA of Kairos Church and an invitation to join us on this exciting adventure of following Jesus. Each section has study questions that are designed to introduce you to the vision and culture of Kairos and to help lay a foundation of discipleship. We are delighted that you are interested in discovering more about the Kairos journey. The adventure starts here.

John and Laura Caldwell

Founding leaders, Kairos Church

VISION AND MISSION

Vision Statement

Kairos Church exists to see all people in Stirling and beyond: **_Encounter Jesus, follow Jesus, and lead_** _others to Jesus._

Encounter Jesus

Our gospel came to you not simply with words but also with power, with the Holy Spirit and deep conviction. (1 Thess 1:5)

Follow Jesus

"Come, follow me," Jesus said, "and I will send you out to fish for people." Matt 4:19

Lead Others

Therefore go and make disciples of all nations, baptizing them in the name of the Father and of the Son and of the Holy Spirit, [20] and teaching them to obey everything I have commanded you. And surely I am with you always, to the very end of the age." Matt 28:19-20

Mission

We have a mission to be a Gospel-centred, Spirit-Filled, God-Glorifying city centre church that boldly preaches the gospel, in the power of the Spirit, reaches the lost, develops disciples, and plants missional churches in Stirling, and beyond.

VISION AND MISSION STUDY QUESTIONS

1. Describe the Kairos vision in your own words (what does it mean to you?)

2. How does the Kairos vision relate to your own calling?

3. Which one of the three parts of the vision (Encounter, Follow, Lead) excites you the most?

4. Which of the three challenges you the most?

5. What does the mission statement mean to you?

6. Would you describe your life as being 'on mission' just now? What areas do you need to grow into? Are you willing to grow in these areas? Write down three action points that will help you grow.

VALUES STATEMENT

K.A.I.R.O.S

Kingdom:

We are a Jesus centred community, where we actively anticipate the manifestation of God's presence and kingdom through worship; preaching and teaching God's Word; the gifts of the Holy Spirit; prayer; and fellowship and unity with all believers.

(Matt 6:10, Heb 12:2a, Col 3:16, Acts 2:42, 1 Pet 4:10, Psalm 29:2)

Authenticity:

We desire to create a culture where people can be honest, without fear of judgement and at the same time encouraging one another to be all that Christ would have us to be. We want to be a people who don't just 'talk the talk' but 'walk the walk.' We believe a grace saturated atmosphere frees us to be honest and empowers us to grow in Christ-like maturity.

(Eph 4:15, 2 Pet 3:18, James 5:16)

Impact:

We believe God wants us to have an impact on the city, communities, family, friends and all who come across our path. Therefore we seek to be led by the Spirit and proactive in our relationships with others in the hope that people encounter the life changing presence of Jesus. Our heart is to raise up, train, and equip every believer to have an impact in their own spheres of influence.

(Rom 8:14, Matt 5:16, 1 Cor 10:31)

Restoration:

We are committed to nurturing an environment of healing, wholeness and recovery for all. We believe there is no such thing as a hopeless case, and that God is in the business of restoring our broken lives.

(2 Cor 13:11, 2 Cor 1:3-4, Psalm 147:3, Isa 61:1)

Outward looking:

We take the call to make disciples seriously. We aim to be a people who proactively engage with the lost to help them discover the love of God and salvation that's freely available through Jesus. God has not called us to a holy huddle of isolation, but to be a missional community of multiplication.

(Matt 28:18-20, Rom 10:14-15, Serving Rom 12:10-11, Col 3:23-24, Phil 2:3-4)

Serving:

We are passionate about creating a welcoming culture that actively honours others through heartfelt hospitality, generosity, and serving. We specifically look for opportunities to serve and support those who are suffering, marginalised, struggling with addiction, and facing times of trauma.

(Rom 12:10-11, Col 3:23-24, Phil 2:3-4)

VALUES QUESTIONS

1. How do you feel about the core values of Kairos? Are these values that you consider to be important?

2. Can you see these values lived out in the life of Jesus?

3. Which values statement/s do you resonate with the most? How might you further develop your passion for this value?

4. Which value statement would you consider to be an area that needs to be developed in your life? How might you grow in this area? Identify three action points that can help you grow in this area.

5. How can we nurture these values in our lives?

6. How could you impact your family, workplace, community, if you were to embody these values?

STRATEGY AND MOTIVATION

Strategy

- Kairos Church aims to create multiple spaces for people to **encounter** Christ through the Word of God, Worship, and the Ministry of the Holy Spirit.
- Kairos Church aims to create a culture and an environment that enables and encourages people to **follow** Jesus and discover the life-transforming process of discipleship.
- Kairos Church aims to equip believers to **lead** others to Christ and to develop disciples who in turn develop other disciples.

Motivation (Why do we do it?)

1. The Glory of God

So, whether you eat or drink, or **whatever you do, do all to the glory of God**. (1 Corinthians 10:31)

2. Obedience to the revealed will of God

Then Jesus came to them and said, "All authority in heaven and on earth has been given to me. Therefore go and make disciples of all nations, baptizing them in the name of the Father and of the Son and of the Holy Spirit, 2 and **teaching them to obey everything I have commanded you.** And surely I am with you always, to the very end of the age." (Matt 28:18-20)

3. Reflecting the compassion and grace of Christ

For **Christ's love compels us**, because we are convinced that one died for all, and therefore all died. 2 Cor. 5:14

How we do it.

- **Creating a culture of Prayer**: the success of our mission and vision is completely dependent upon a spirit of prayer, intimacy, and intercession. **Prayer prepares the way for encounter.**
- **Collective Worship**: the primary context for encounter is the collective worship environment where the Word is preached, prayers are offered, the sacraments administered, and the scriptures are read.
- **Preaching the Gospel**: It is the gospel which brings people into an encounter with Jesus Christ. The only way unbelievers will encounter God, is ultimately through hearing the gospel, and repenting and believing and receiving the Holy Spirit. Confidence in the power of the gospel is the primary means of achieving our vision.

- **Leadership Development**: Identifying, developing and releasing leaders to use their gifts and fulfil their calling.
- **Prayer Ministry:** Regular opportunities for prayer ministry for healing, prophecy, and encouragement.
- **Small groups** are at the heart of the Kairos vision and strategy. Small groups (Discovery Groups) are at the heart of the Kairos vision. Through small groups we nurture discipleship, mission and develop leaders. Small groups are not an activity of the church, they are the church. Small groups are not limited to Stirling, and whenever there is an opportunity to plant a small group in another locality, the aim should be to help see that group multiply and transition into a local congregation.
- **Dependence on the presence and power of the Holy Spirit**. Only the Holy Spirit can lead us into an encounter with Christ. Only the Holy Spirit can enable us to follow Jesus. And only the Holy Spirit can empower us to make disciples who make disciples. We actively pursue the fullness of the Holy Spirit.
- **Creating spaces** for unbelievers to meet Christians, hear the gospel, receive prayer, and experience Christ through the believer as Christians minister to non-Christians in *word and deed.* (Small groups, 1-2-1s,

evangelistic events, social events etc.)

- **Individual believers** are encouraged and **inspired to create spaces** for encounter through their **daily lives**, as they **connect with neighbours, friends, and colleagues**. Believers should be equipped to recognise opportunities to manifest the fruit of the Spirit, move in the gifts of the Spirit, and to share personal testimony, and the gospel of Jesus Christ in a real, relevant and non-threatening way. Creating spaces for encounter can be as simple as taking time for a conversation, or going for a coffee, or seeking ways to serve friends and neighbours.

Success Indicators

- Church is engaging with/connecting with unbelievers and non-Christians are engaging with the church services, small groups, events etc.
- People are placing their faith in Christ.
- People are encountering Christ.
- People are being baptised.
- People are growing in discipleship (faith, prayer, love, holiness, hope, relationships, the gifts of the Spirit and serving)
- Individuals are connecting/engaging with unbelievers in their daily lives (evidenced by testimonies).
- Individual believers are leading people to Christ and discipling them.
- Leaders/ministries are being recognised, raised up, developed and released.
- Small groups are being established and are multiplying.
- People testify to healing/help.
- Individuals are proactively practicing hospitality for both people who are part of Kairos and those who are not.
- Individuals are proactively serving believers and unbelievers in practical ways.
- Individuals are actively supporting the vision of Kairos through Tithes and Offerings.

STRATEGY AND MOTIVATION QUESTIONS

1. Do you feel your own gifts and calling align with the Kairos strategy? Which areas do you connect with the most?

2. Which areas of the Kairos strategy do you least connect with? How might you grow in those areas of serving? Jot down three action points that can help you grow in these areas.

3. What do you think about the Kairos motivations for ministry? Are these your motivations for serving God? Do you think we can have a wrong motivation for serving? What are some unhealthy motivations for serving? How can we develop healthy motivations for serving God?

4. Have a look at the 'success indicators' (engaging with unbelievers, engaging in small groups, growing in gifts and character etc), if we think of these as

the fruit of discipleship, can you see some fruit in your own life? Are there areas of fruitfulness you need to grow? How might you begin to develop these areas? Write down three action points that could help you grow.

WHAT WE BELIEVE

1. The one true and living God who eternally exists in three persons in unity: Father, Son and Holy Spirit. Genesis 1:1; Matt 3:16-17; 1 John 5:7

2. The inherent corruptness of man through the Fall; The necessity of repentance and regeneration by grace and through faith in Christ alone and the eternal separation from God of the finally unrepentant. Gen 3:1-19; Isaiah 53:6; Acts 2:38; 17:30, John 5:28-29; Daniel 12:2; Romans 2:7, 6:23; 1 John 1:1-2

3. The Virgin birth, sinless life, atoning death, triumphant resurrection, ascension and continuing intercession of our Lord Jesus Christ; His second coming and millennial reign upon earth. John 8:46; 14:30; Col. 1:15; 2 Corinthians 5:19; Romans 3:25; Acts 2:36; Phil. 2:9-11; 1 Thessalonians 4:16-17; Rev. 22:20

4. Justification and sanctification of the believer through the finished work of Christ. Acts 2:38; Luke 15:7; Romans 4:25; 5:16; 1 Corinthians 1:30; 1 Thessalonians

4:30

5. The baptism of the Holy spirit for believers with supernatural signs, empowering the church for its mission in the world. 1 Corinthians 12:8-11; Mark 16:17; Acts 2:4; and Galatians 5:22

6. The gifts of the Holy Spirit for the building up of the Church and ministry to the world..1 Corinthians 12:4-11

7. The sacraments of baptism by immersion and of the Lord's Supper. Rom 6:4, 6:11, 6:13-14, Luke 3:21; Mark 16:16, Luke 2:22-24, 34; Mark 10:16, Luke 22:19-20; Matt. 26:21-29; Acts 20:7

8. The divine inspiration and authority of the Holy Scriptures. 2 Tim 3:16, 2 Peter 1:21

9. Christ's leadership of the Church through apostles, prophets, evangelists, pastors, teachers, elders and deacons, for unity, maturity and growth of the church. Ephesians 4:11-13, 1 Corinthians 12:28

10. The security of the believer as he remains in Christ. 1 Corinthians 10:12, 1 John 5:11, John 15:4, 1 John 5:12, Romans 5:1-2, John 8:51, 1 Timothy 4:1, 16; 2 Timothy 3:13-15, 1 Corinthians 15:1, Colossians 1:21-23

11. The privilege and responsibility of bringing tithes and offerings to the Lord. Malachi 3:10, Matthew 23:23, Hebrews 7:1-4; Luke 6:38; Acts 20:35

WHAT WE BELIEVE QUESTIONS

1. Read through each of the core beliefs and the accompanying scriptures and take notes on anything you learn or don't understand.

2. Are there any beliefs or scriptures you find confusing or hard to accept?

3. What is your understanding of the new birth (regeneration)?

4. What role should the scriptures (The Word of God) have in your life? Are you actively seeking to learn and live the Word of God? What might help you engage more effectively with the Word of God?

5. What should we do if the Bible contradicts our thinking, beliefs or behaviours?

6. Have you experienced the filling and empowering of the Holy Spirit?

7. Do you feel you can align yourself with the church's teaching?

8. Up until now, how do you understand the

Bible's teachings on financial stewardship?

9. Are you willing to apply the Bible's teaching on financial stewardship, and supporting the local church financially, as part of your worship and discipleship?

10. Are you committed to growing and developing as a disciple (follower of Jesus) and invite church leaders to support, nurture and hold you accountable?

SPIRITUAL HEALTH CHECK

This is for your own personal reflection, but you may want to talk these areas through with a trusted believer, mentor, small group leader or pastor.

For each question answer the following:

- Yes/No/In process.

- How can I do this/continue to develop this?

1. Have I repented of my sins, placed my faith in Jesus as my Lord and Saviour?

2. Am I regularly praying and reading the Bible?

3. Am I regularly attending Sunday Worship?

4. Am I invested in a small group?

5. Am I actively serving the church?

6. Am I honouring the Lord and supporting the ministry through regular tithes and

offerings?

7. Am I proactively seeking to overcome sin in my life, and live with integrity and righteousness?

8. Am I growing in my knowledge of essential doctrines?

9. Am I actively living out the church's vision and mission to connect with those who don't know Jesus?

YOUR VISION

What are some of the things that you would love to see God do for you, in you and through you by this time next year? (Think in terms of healing, equipping, relationship with God, gifts, callings, life goals etc.)

How can Kairos help you towards this vision?

What do you need to do to make this vision a reality?

Next Steps

Having completed this short course, what are your next steps to help you grow as a disciple?

Here are some suggestions:

- Spend daily time with God.
- Join a small group.
- Speak to your pastor about hosting or leading a small group.
- Get involved in serving.
- Talk with your pastor about starting a new ministry.
- Find an accountability partner.
- Open your home for hospitality.
- Begin to share your faith with unbelievers.
- Begin to invite people to small group or church.
- Start to honour the Lord through Biblical financial stewardship, by supporting the local church through tithes and offerings.
- Cut out any known sin in your life.
- Pray for your leaders.
- Other suggestions?

Printed in Great Britain
by Amazon

36275471R10020